THE KIRK YETHOLM GYPSIES

A. V. TOKELY

Copyright © 2004 by
A. V. Tokely

The right of A. V. Tokely to be identified as the Author of the Work has been asserted by him in accordance with the Copyright, Design and Patents Act 1988.

All photographs are from the Tokely family collection.

Printed and bound by Buccleuch Printers, Hawick,
with support from
Hawick Archaeological Society.

ISBN 0 9518647 2 6

CONTENTS

Foreword	vii
Introduction	ix
The Kirk Yetholm Gypsies	1
Village Life	5
The Gypsy Royal Family:	
Jean Gordon and Patrick Faa	11
King Will Faa I	17
King Will Faa II	19
King Charles Blyth I	22
Queen Esther	25
King Charles Faa Blyth II	31
Prince Robert	37
Food	39
Fighting	42
Language	45
Religion	47
Fairs	53
Gypsy Characters:	
Madge Gordon	56
Jock Blythe	63
John Tait (Stovie Jock)	67
Andrew Blythe	78
Bibliography	83
Appendix	84

A. V. Tokely

FOREWORD

Vic was born and raised in the village of Town Yetholm, just a quarter century after the death of King Charles Faa Blyth. He grew up in an environment rich in Gypsy folklore, among those with whom the Kirk Yetholm Gypsies lived, worked and socialised. Indeed, his grandfather was one of the escorts at the King's coronation in 1898. Vic inherited a fond regard for the Gypsy culture of the day – a fascination that was to span his whole life.

A man of many interests, Vic was a keen sportsman, playing football, cricket, running, and in his later years, golf and bowling, though his greatest passion was always fishing. Though a reserved and gentle man by nature, he had a flair for public speaking and his profound knowledge of Border history resulted in him being called upon to give many talks to audiences around the Borders and on TV. There were many facets of the rich Border history that Vic held dear to his heart, including the poetry of Will Ogilvie and the Battle of Flodden. However, it was for his knowledge and synergy with the Kirk Yetholm Gypsy history that he was renowned worldwide as the leading authority. My grandmother, like her great-grandmother Queen Esther Faa

Blyth before her, had a profound depth of character. It was her stories and references to the Gypsy characters that kindled my desire to know more of my ancestry. Vic kindly started me on the path of an ever-increasing and fascinating discovery. Since then, I have read many articles, both historic and current, regarding the Kirk Yetholm Gypsies, and in particular Queen Esther and her family. There are few texts I have read which encapsulate the spirit of the Royal Gypsies quite as Vic did.

Sadly, Vic passed away before he could see this book published. It was a pleasure to have known him, to have shared his knowledge and to be in his company during my regular pilgrimages to Kirk Yetholm. At the time of those visits, Vic spoke of his wish to see a memorial stone in Kirk Yetholm, to commemorate the Kirk Yetholm Gypsies of years gone by. I am delighted to say that such a memorial now stands on The Green in Kirk Yetholm village, thanks to a generous donation from Blinkbonny Quarry. It also marks the contribution Vic Tokely made in keeping the story alive.

Janet Fletcher

INTRODUCTION

It is satisfying to see this book finished, but disappointing that we are unable to say 'complete'. Unfortunately, Dad's illness meant it was not possible for him to complete his book as he had planned. There are many gaps which he would have gone on to fill and points that he would have researched more deeply if he had been able. We don't have the expertise to fill those gaps, and hope readers will understand this. This book stands as a reminder of Dad's many inspiring lectures over the years, and aims to ensure that his knowledge, research and colourful anecdotes about the Kirk Yetholm Gypsies aren't lost.

One aspect which we feel makes the book different and unique to others in its field is the way it captures many of the characters that existed in the Gypsy tribe of Kirk Yetholm. This is important because it gives a feel of personality, of wit and humour which is vital in preserving memories forever. We are fortunate that this has been part of our own lives, because our dad was a true character.

We feel indebted to Jules Horne for her guidance on this book. We would also like to thank Hawick Archaeological

Society for their help in funding its publication, as well as Tom Tokely and Janet Fletcher for their indispensable contributions.

Anne Scott
Jill Latta

THE KIRK YETHOLM GYPSIES

The Gypsies arrived in Scotland in around 1500, having made the long tortuous journey from India. They were well received in Scotland, and their conduct was regulated by their own tribal leaders, who administered justice as was required.

In 1506, King James IV wrote to the King of Denmark, informing him that a tribe of people called Gypsies or Egyptians were touring Scotland on instructions from the Pope.

The Gypsies' conduct in the 16th and early 17th centuries became unacceptable, so much so that in 1609, an Act of Parliament decreed that any Gypsy found in Scotland was to be hung, and Gypsy women drowned.

On 31st July 1611, four gypsies were hung on the Boroughmuir, not for any misdemeanour, but for being Gypsies and having remained in Scotland.

To save their lives, the Gypsies did a number of things:

    (a)   fell in with the inhabitants' way of life
    (b)   changed their dress to that worn by Scots

(c) changed their names to those of local people
(d) intermarried with local inhabitants
(e) kidnapped Scots children and brought them up as their own
(f) moved to areas such as the Borders, where they could seek refuge in the Cheviot Hills, or over into England.

The Gypsies wandered around the Borders in all types of weather, and it was no surprise when a number of the lads took the King's shilling and joined the army.

There were a number of Gypsies in the company commanded by the Laird of Kirk Yetholm, Captain Bennet. At the Battle of Namur in 1695, one of the Gypsy lads saved the Captain's life. As a reward for this brave act, the Captain provided houses in Kirk Yetholm for that Gypsy and his friends.

The houses were feued or rented to the Gypsies at a 1/- per year, and the leases were for 19 x 19 years. The let consisted of a cottage, garden at the back of the house and about a quarter of an acre of land on the loaning – a stretch of cultivated land adjacent to the village. In the same direction as the loaning, towards the English Border, was about 200 acres of common land on which the Kirk Yetholm residents were allowed to graze a cow, a horse, donkey, cuddy or pownie[1], besides being allowed to cut peats.

The first Gypsy settlers were the Youngs, Taits, Gordons, Fleckies, Douglas and Blyths. Dark curly hair, dark eyes, high cheekbones, and olive or tawny skin was their general

---
[1] Pony.

appearance, excepting the Blyths, who had blue eyes and fair hair.

The practice of giving people nicknames was prevalent years ago, and in Kirk Yetholm this was probably necessary, with as many as seven Douglas families, each with a son called Matthew. They were therefore referred to by names such as 'blind Mathy wi the stick' or 'Mathy o'er the Green'.

Kirk Yetholm has been referred to as the home of the Kings of the Scottish Gypsies, but this is doubtful. The home of the Gypsy King of South East Scotland would be more accurate.

From earliest times to the last crowning, the Royal Family have been related or connected with the surname of Faa. The Faas or Falls of Dunbar considered themselves to be descended from the Kirk Yetholm Gypsies. Mrs. Fall of Dunbar, whose husband was the Provost of Dunbar in the early 1700s, depicted her whole family in needlework or tapestry with their asses, as they took their departure from Yetholm.

An old Berwickshire gentleman, who had the account from his mother, said that on their departure from Kirk Yetholm, the Falls stopped some little time at Hume in Berwickshire, where they had some female relations. After a few days there, they set out for Dunbar, taking their female friends with them.

There are a number of questions on the appearance of the name of Faa or Fall in the area. The Gypsies were first reported to be in Kirk Yetholm in about 1695. The Gypsies of Dunbar consider themselves to be descended from the Kirk Yetholm Gypsies, previously described.

However, there was a Thomas Fall in Dunbar in 1400, Alexander Fall in 1419, and Sir David Faw in 1451.

Were these people in the 1400s not Gypsies? Did the Gypsies assume their names, as they did with other Scots people, such as the Douglases and Youngs? Or did the Gypsies come to Scotland earlier than has been stated in records?

Sir John Anstruther, much to the displeasure of those in his society, married a Gypsy, Jenny Faa, who was a great beauty. When she appeared in Dunbar, the local population burst into singing *'Gypsy Laddie'*, with the intention of humbling the lady and reminding her of her lowly origins. She was not dispirited by such actions, and smiled at their efforts to belittle her.

The Kirk Yetholm Gypsies considered they were related to Johnnie Faa, who stole the Earl of Cassillis' lady, as told in the well-known ballad[2].

---

[2] See Appendix.

VILLAGE LIFE

The Young family of Kirk Yetholm, early 1900s

In the early days, the local inhabitants looked with disdain on the Gypsy men's attitude to earning a living, where the Gypsy women did most of the work. One old Gypsy stated, 'Man, a'm no lazy, but a dinnae heed aboot work.'

There were a number who repaired pots and pans, and made small metal objects known as trinkets.

A few – known as 'horners' – made spoons from the horns of sheep. I remember as a wee laddie taking sago pudding (which I detested) with a horn spoon at my Grannie's. My Grandfather had a small farm in Yetholm, and Grannie would say, 'Thae

Gypsy kind frae Kirk Yetholm would cadge some hay frae your Grandfather and give him twae or three horn spoons in payment.'

They would say: 'A hae nought to cairry the hay, Jim,' and would make a hay rope in which to carry the hay, since there was more hay in the rope than the loose hay which they carried away.

Generally, the Gypsies were potters or muggers, making and selling baskets, brushes, doormats, and fancy goods. Bartering was greatly practised, and they displayed great skill in obtaining bargains.

It was the women who did the selling. With their persuasive tongue and fearful threatening attitudes, they did good business.

Like many country people in days gone by, they lived off the land, hunting, fishing and shooting, applying their skills by fair means or foul to obtain food for the pot.

A good lurcher dog was kept to catch rabbits, hares and feathered game which tarried too late on the ground. The Gypsies, like most predators, did not go hungry too often.

Whenever I read Sir Walter Scott's novel, *Guy Mannering*, about Meg Merrilees, the Gypsy – lifting the lid of her cauldron, which contained fowls, hares, partridges and moor game, boiled with potatoes, onions and leeks – I recall an occasion when an old Gypsy invited my brothers and self to partake of a similar feast. I was the only one to accept the invitation, and despite the predictions by my brothers of an early death by poisoning, I look back on the occasion, sure that the memory of the potage improves with the passing years.

The wealth of the Gypsies at the time was measured not in money, but in the number of donkeys and horses he owned. The Gypsy had a natural gift for horse trading, and knew best how to prepare a horse for the sale ring. They were at their best at fairs such as Boswells. Unsound horses were trotted up and down prior to being offered for sale, so that their limbs were warmed up and made to appear sound. Young men could be seen riding bareback with horses unbridled, and only a halter for guidance.

Steps were taken to try and cure pownies which had some malady. There was a small, smart quality pownie in Kirk Yetholm which had but one fault: it was frightened by unusual noises. The two brothers in joint ownership agreed they would have to try and cure this malady. They decided that one would trot up the road mounted, while the other jumped out, making a noise. On the agreed day, the pownie and rider came trotting up the road at a great lick, when a body jumped out from the side of the road shouting 'boof!' The pownie shied sharply, threw its rider and trotted on into the distance. The dislodged rider gathered himself up from the hard road, vented his fury on his brother and exclaimed: 'It was a guy big boof for a little wee pownie'.

Gypsies are often associated with fortune telling – a practice in which many of the females were and are gifted. Queen Esther was said to be a 'spaewife' – a teller of the future.

A visiting minister to Town Yetholm informed the local blacksmith that he was to have his fortune told by the Queen. At this information, the blacksmith became extremely interested in the minister's past life: it appeared he had been married on two previous occasions, and had with him his girlfriend. The blacksmith and Queen Esther were 'guy thick'[3], it was said, and it was a veritable feast of information that was fed to the Queen on the minister's past. Quite naturally, on the appointed day, the minister was flabbergasted by Queen Esther's pronouncements. She ended by saying: 'Eh, minister, ye are a guid man, but an affy waster o women'.

The Gypsies were strong characters and, if trusted, would never deceive, nor forfeit their promise. A lawyer in Jedburgh said that he would rather trust a Gypsy before ten ordinary people. Kindness was long remembered, and trusting farmers on whose land Gypsies camped would never lose hens, ducks or sheep. In fact, they became guardians and kept vigil on local people who were tempted to pilfer from farmers. However, they were fierce enemies, as Old Will of Phaup, grandfather of James Hogg, the Ettrick Shepherd, experienced when he thrashed a Gypsy for illegally grazing horses on prime grass. Eventually a truce was arranged, or Will was almost certain to be ruined.

They were extremely witty, and seldom came off worst in an argument. One day, walking through the village, the local minister asked the Gypsy lads gathered at the street corner what they were talking about.

One Gypsy lad said: 'We are trying to discover the difference between two words.'

'Oh, yes? What are they?' said the minister.

'Remember and recollect,' replied the Gypsy lad.

---

[3] Close.

'Why do you want to know?' asked the minister.

'I remember making a basket for you, but I can't recollect getting paid for it,' replied the Gypsy.

The last Gypsy Palace in Kirk Yetholm, early 1900s

In the early days, the houses around the Green were built with the gable ends facing inwards, and were thatched with rushes and straw. They were poorly furnished and untidy, and livestock often made their appearance in the passage to the living quarters.

The green, encased by houses on all sides, was a haven for all and sundry: horses, pownies, donkeys, carts, floats, dogs of all breeds and cross-breeds, and to add to the confusion, pigs and hens scratched about on middens. The green was the playground for the children, and the scene of high jinks in the evenings, when the Gypsies played at football and settled their differences, occasionally fortified by drink.

These houses were occupied only during the winter months, and at the first call of spring, they would be closed up, and the Gypsies would set off on their travels around their prescribed area, which went as far west as Langholm, up into the Lothians, to Berwickshire, the Borders and Northumberland. Camps would be set up on old roads, loanings, near plantations, or by old disused buildings near or on farms.

It was the practice of the Gypsies to camp at the same place each year. Mellerstain Entries near Earlston was a popular camping place, having good facilities for food and drink, and within easy reach of farms and villages to sell their wares.

THE GYPSY ROYAL FAMILY
JEAN GORDON AND PATRICK FAA

Jean Gordon (c. 1670 – 1746) and her husband Patrick Faa (c. 1670 – 1727), although not mentioned as kings and queens, were certainly the first leaders of the Kirk Yetholm Gypsies. Jean, it was said, stood six feet tall, had raven black hair which hung around her shoulders, an aquiline nose, piercing eyes, wore a cloak and a man's overcoat, and on all occasions carried a large staff, which was threateningly wielded to add to her reputation of being savage and fearsome. She had a commanding and queenly presence, and was greatly respected.

Sir Walter Scott said she was quite a Meg Merrilees, and was a strong influence in depicting that character in his book, *Guy Mannering*, although her granddaughter, Madge, had similar features and characteristics. Sir Walter had met Madge as a boy, when she called on his father for her awmous[4]. So most probably, the character of Meg Merrilees was drawn from both Jean and Madge Gordon.

'Having been often hospitably received at the farm-house of Lochside, near Yetholm, she had carefully abstained from

---
[4] Alms.

committing any depredations on the farmer's property. But it seems that her sons (nine in number) did not have the same delicacy, and stole a brood-sow from their kind entertainer.

'Jean was so much mortified at this ungrateful conduct, and so much ashamed of it, that she absented herself from Lochside for several years. At length, in consequence of some temporary pecuniary necessity, the good-man of Lochside was obliged to go to Newcastle, to get some money to pay his rent. Returning through the mountains of Cheviot, he was benighted, and lost his way.

'A light, glimmering through the window of a large waste-barn, which had survived the farm-house to which it had once belonged, guided him to a place of shelter; and when he knocked at the door, it was opened by Jean Gordon. Her very remarkable figure, for she was nearly six feet high, and her equally remarkable features and dress, made it impossible to mistake her for a moment; and to meet with such a character, in so solitary a place, and probably at no great distance from her clan, was a terrible surprise to the poor man, whose rent (to lose which would have been ruin to him) was about his person.

'Jean set up a loud shout of joyful recognition.

'"Eh, sirs! The winsome gude-man of Lochside! Light down, light down; for ye manna gang farther the night, and a friend's house sae near!"

'The farmer was obliged to dismount, and accept the Gypsy's offer of supper and a bed. There was plenty of meat in the barn, however it might be come by, and preparations were going on for a plentiful supper, which the farmer, to the great increase of his anxiety, observed was calculated for ten or twelve guests of the same description, no doubt, with his landlady. Jean left him in no doubt on the subject. She brought up the story of the stolen sow, and noticed how much pain and vexation it had given her. Like other philosophers, she remarked that the world grows worse daily, and, like other parents, that the bairns got out of her guiding, and neglected the old Gypsy regulations which commanded them to respect, in their depredations, the property of their benefactors.

'The end of all this was an enquiry what money the farmer had about him, and an urgent request that he would make her his purse-keeper, as the bairns, as she called her sons, would be soon home. The poor farmer made a virtue of necessity, told his story, and surrendered his gold to Jean's custody. She made him put a few shillings in his pocket; observing it would excite suspicion should he be found travelling altogether penniless. This arrangement being made, the farmer lay down on a sort of shake-down, as the Scotch call it, upon some straw; but, as is easily to be believed, slept not.

'About midnight the gang returned with various articles of plunder, and talked over their exploits, in language which made the farmer tremble. They were not long in discovering their guest, and demanded of Jean whom she had got there.

'"E'en the winsome gude-man of Lochside, poor boy," replied Jean. "He's been at Newcastle, seeking siller to pay his rent, honest man, but deil-be-licket he's been able to gather in; and sae he's gaun e'en hame wi' a toom purse and a sair heart."

'"That may be, Jean," replied one of the banditti, but we

maun rip his pouches a bit, and see if it be true or no."

'Jean set up her throat in exclamation against this breach of hospitality, but without producing any change of their determination. The farmer soon heard their stifled whispers and light steps by his bed-side, and understood they were rummaging his clothes. When they found the money which the prudence of Jean Gordon had made him retain, they held a consultation if they should take it or not; but the smallness of the booty, and the vehemence of Jean's remonstrances, determined them on the negative. They caroused, and went to rest.

'So soon as day dawned, Jean roused her guest, produced his horse, which she had accommodated behind the hallan, and guided him for some miles, till he was on the high-road to Lochside. She then restored his whole property, nor could his earnest entreaties prevail on her to accept so much as a single guinea.'[5]

It was the practice of the Gypsies when travelling around the countryside to ask the farmer for shelter and to barter for a hen, but some Gypsies merely deposited themselves on a farm and took a hen or some other item of food. This practice was known as 'sorning'. It may be asked why resistance was not offered against this imposition, but as some of the Gypsies were armed with swords and pistols, it was difficult to show objection.

However, in 1714, Sir William Kerr of Bridgend House, Kelso – a magistrate in the Court of Jedburgh – decided to put an end to this practice. He arranged for the arrest of Patrick

[5] Sir Walter Scott. *Guy Mannering*. London: Dent. 1906

Faa, Jean Gordon and a number of the tribe, and had them imprisoned in the jail at Jedburgh.

Patrick Faa's mother, Janet Stewart (referred to by her maiden name), pleaded unsuccessfully with Sir William Kerr for their release. The distraught mother was even further upset when farm workers falsely and maliciously told her that news circulating suggested that those in custody were to be hung after the sitting of the next Circuit Court. Within a few days, Bridgend House was burned down.

Janet Stewart was taken into custody. Although no firm evidence could be levelled against her, she was scourged by the common hangman, receiving four stripes at the Townfoot, the Market Cross and the West Post. She was nailed by the ear to a post erected at the Market Cross for a quarter of an hour.

Her son, Patrick had both his ears cut off for scriving[6]. Along with the other accused, he was deported to one of Queen Anne's plantations in the Indies. Jean was left on her own to bring up the family.

Jean and Patrick had a family of three daughters and nine sons. One of the sons was murdered, five were hung for sheep stealing, and the last three of her sons were on trial at Jedburgh in 1730 for sheep stealing. The jury decided by a majority of one that they were guilty. Jean is reported to have called from the public benches: 'The Lord help the innocent on a day like this.'

Jean's turbulent life was brought to a close in Carlisle, when she gave vent to her support for Bonnie Prince Charlie. In retribution, the market crowd ducked and drowned her in the

---

[6] Thieving

River Eden. Her last words were said to be 'Chairlie yet, Chairlie yet'.

Sir Walter Scott said: 'When a child, and among the scene she frequented, I have often heard these stories, and cried piteously for poor Jean Gordon.'

It was Keats who wrote:

> *'Old Meg she was a Gypsy*
> > *And liv'd upon the Moors:*
> *Her bed it was the brown heath turf*
> > *And her house was out of doors.*
>
> *Her brothers were the craggy hills,*
> > *Her sisters larchen trees–*
> *Alone with her great family*
> > *She liv'd as she did please.*[7]

---

[7] John Keats. *Poetical Works*. Oxford: OUP, 1970.

KING WILL FAA I

Reign 1746 – 1784

Will Faa became King in 1746, and was said to have been married three times and had 24 children. All were baptised by Mr. Leck, the local minister. Because of a twist in his throat, Will was nicknamed 'Gleed Neckit Will'.

These christenings were held in the church, and the mother was attended by two young girls called 'kimmers', who were supplied with bread and cheese. Their duty was to give some to the first person they met. Many of the local dignitaries attended the christenings, which were followed by a lavish feast.

Will was highly respected and guarded the house of the laird, Mr. Nisbet of Marlefield, when he was away from home. Being so trustworthy, he was given the keys of the house. He was the restorer of stolen goods, or 'country keeper', as it was called, and often a stolen horse would be recovered in a few days after Will had scoured the countryside.

On one occasion, Will accosted the minister with a view to robbery as he returned from Northumberland by the Staw road, which ran near Kirk Yetholm Mains. He was shocked and apologetic when he realised it was the local minister.

In later years, hearing that Mr. Nisbet, the Laird, was seriously ill at Dirleton, Will made the trip to wish him well. After carrying on to view Edinburgh, he returned by the coast to as far as Coldingham, where he suddenly took ill and died.

There were over 300 donkeys and many mourners in the funeral cortege to Kirk Yetholm. In the usual way, the wake after the internment lasted three days, with much eating and drinking.

KING WILL FAA II

Reign 1784 –1847

On the death of his father, the eldest son, Will, was crowned king, but had to struggle to maintain the 'crown'. He was opposed by one of a lesser tribe called the 'Earl of Hell', who fought against Will and his followers on the Green.

Will was broad shouldered, strong and of athletic build. He had the reputation of being a pugilist of some ability, and was greatly feared and respected in this field.

He competed in the sports and games, and especially at the Fastern E'en games. This was a great day of sports and 'Baa' playing. The latter was played on the haugh between the two villages, by the married and single men. Kirk Yetholm men and women – mostly Gypsies – played against those 'frae the toon'.

On one occasion, it became so fierce that the Gypsies locked their doors when the Yetholmites threatened violence. One king took down his sword and said that a few heids would roll if those 'frae ower the witter' tried to gain access. Generally, they retired to the inns, where they ate currant dumplings and pancakes, and drank extensively.

Over the years, there have been athletes from Yetholm of great ability, besides Will Faa II. At the first Powderhall sprint, held in 1870, the 'back marker' or scratch runner was one by the name of Carruthers, who came from Yetholm. Billy Elliot from 'the back o' the Hill' (Halterburn) won the Powderhall mile event in two successive years in the 1960s.

I went to the Border Shepherds' Show about 20 years ago in the morning. As I journeyed 'doon the toon' I met the oldest man in the village, and the biggest character – 'Little Ritchie', as he was known.

'Hello son. Are ye doon for the show?'

'Aye. Just for a wee while, Ritchie.'

'Whae's yon coming up the toon, Ritchie?'

'Ah, a dinnae ken, son. A think hai's a white settler.'

'Man, look at the way hais legs are gan. There's no knee bones.'

'Are ye gan tae the show, Ritchie?'

'Gan tae the show, son? A wudnae miss it, man. A div like the rinnin.'

'Are there mony guid rinners aboot Yetholm the now?'

'Man, there's never been a guid rinner came oot o' Yetholm since they shifted the polis tae Kelsae.'

―――――

To return to Will II: he earned a living carting coals to Kelso and Jedburgh in winter time, and in tent life travelled extensively, selling bits of pottery, brushes, etc.

He was involved in the smuggling trade, taking whisky over the Border into Northumberland. There was a tax on whisky going out of Scotland and, since there were two distilleries in Yetholm as well as a number of illicit distilleries up Bowmont Water, the contraband trade was profitable and lively.

The risk and profit of the trade appealed to Will. However, an excise officer caught up with him. In the ensuing 'battle' – Will armed with a cudgel, his adversary with a sword – Will came off worst, having his hand severely damaged. Will was an accomplished fiddler, and philosophically remarked that Scotland had lost one of its greatest fiddlers.

Will did not stay in the old Palace[8], but was the landlord of the Queen Inn, and was foremost in all the cracks, relating his feats in his youth. He was a man of the world and a shrewd one, profiting at every chance. He had the privilege of shooting and fishing around the countryside, and had great ability in this sporting field.

He displayed his profession with a selection of coloured flies in his hat, and there is no doubt he had great ability in taking trout, by fair means or foul.

Will lived until he was 96 and, as he had no family, was succeeded by his brother-in-law.

---

[8] Now 'Burnside', on the Green in Kirk Yetholm.

KING CHARLES BLYTH I

Reign 1847 – 1861

The next King was Charles Blyth, brother-in-law of Will Faa II. He was crowned in 1847 at the age of 69, and was greatly respected in the village and the surrounding district.

George Gladstone, the local blacksmith, performed the ceremony. The crowd called 'Long live Charles the First' after drinking His Majesty's health, and the other royal toasts. The cavalcade then moved out to the common, where a long-tailed white horse was in readiness for His Majesty, and three or four bottles of whisky were quaffed. The procession then proceeded round the marches of the Common in the following order:

The King upon his white palfrey, led by two grooms, attendants, retainers, followed by his squire mounted upon a donkey, then the crowd behind. In going down a hill, some of His Majesty's men, more merry than wise, kept tickling the horse behind. Thus disturbed, the horse broke away from the grooms and Charles the First embraced his mother earth.

Dr. Turner, who was present, felt the pulse of the King and prescribed a glass of whisky, after which the King gradually recovered. To give expression to the general joy at the harmless result of the accident, the band struck up a merry tune, and a lady and gentleman of the court danced a jig upon the turf.

After His Majesty was once again mounted, a hare was raised which, being pursued by the royal retinue, was quickly run down. The procession was again formed and marched on to the Stob Stane, where a halt was made. The King dismounted from the palfrey and got up on the stone with the captured hare hung around his neck as a trophy of game from the Gypsy common. Whilst the merry monarch was seated there, his royal head was anointed with whisky instead of oil, and his health again toasted, amidst tremendous cheering.

The procession then returned to the village where Royal honours were again bestowed upon the King, the band playing 'Welcome Royal Charlie'. The royal party went into Mrs Govanlock's Inn and enjoyed themselves in the rollicking style of the Gypsies.

Born in Yorkshire, Charles Blyth I earned a living by selling earthenware and bits of finery. He was well read and amassed a great deal of information on nature and life and, being shrewd, talked a great deal of sense.

He was friendly with Sir Walter Scott, who enjoyed conversing with him whilst encamped near Abbotsford. Sir Walter gleaned much information on the Gypsy character and ways of life. Sir Walter said he was happiest in the company of Gypsies and people of the ordinary stations of life, rather than lords and ladies and those of high rank.

In the early years, Charles saw to it that his children were educated, and assisted Rev. John Baird in carrying out his education programme for the benefit of the Gypsy children in particular.

He maintained the position as King with the conduct and bearing befitting such a high station, but with little income to support him. The benevolence of visitors and, in particular, Lady John Scott of Spottiswoode, who gifted him bits of silver regularly, helped the old King to enjoy a few additional pleasures in his latter days. The presence of his youngest daughter Helen, who attended to his physical requirements, and the spiritual uplift of the Bible, did much to comfort him. He died at the age of 83, having reigned 14 years.

QUEEN ESTHER

Reign 1861 – 1883

Queen Esther

When Charles Blyth died, it was expected that his youngest daughter would become Queen, in view of the fact that she had nursed him in his declining years in the old Palace, which was situated opposite the Tinkers' Row.

King David left both male and female issue, and the eldest son, David, had no wish to become King. He hoped that his youngest sister, Princess Helen, nicknamed 'Black-Bearded Nell', would assume the duties and responsibilities of the throne.

But eldest sister Esther protested against the proposed election on the grounds of seniority and the fact that she was a Faa – Esther Faa Blyth.

Helen was not too sure of her claim to the throne, but placed great reliance on the fact that she was the sole owner and occupier of the Palace. However, when she left Kirk Yetholm on a visit to friends for a few days, her elder sister quickly appeared on the scene and started to canvas for election to the throne. It would seem she was successful, as she gained plenty of support.

It was agreed to put the matter to the vote. Fastern E'en was the appointed day for the voting to take place. However, Helen did not appear to stake her claim, so Esther was appointed Queen.

On 19th November 1861, she was proclaimed Queen at the Market Cross, in the presence of a great assembly. The crowner, the blacksmith George Gladstone from Town Yetholm, read from a scroll that he had the right to crown her, as he had crowned her father some 14 years before. In placing the crown on her head, he shouted out 'challenge who dare'.

In a brief speech, the Queen expressed the hope that her subjects would be peace-loving and law-abiding. A generous amount of whisky was handed round and the assembly drank heavily and heartily to the health and happiness of Her Majesty.

A tour of the inns followed, and then a dance on the Green o' Kirk Yetholm, which was curtailed by rain.

Queen Esther was a woman of great eloquence, especially when her temper was up. She said that she had to have 50 faces, a face for the minister and a face for the blackguard.

She had many sayings: *'A man may care and still be bare if his wife be nought; a man may spend and have money to lend if his wife be ought.'*

On being asked which was the better of the two villages, she replied: 'Kirk Yetholm – it has the Parish Kirk, the wool manufactory and me'.

Like most of the Gypsies, she smoked the clay pipe. It helped to clear her tubes, as she would say. On her wanderings, she wore a scarlet robe of state, a purple hood and sometimes a purple jacket and elastic-sided boots.

Esther was the eldest daughter of Charles, and received a certain amount of education, which for a Gypsy female was unusual.

She married John Rutherford – named 'Jethart Jock' in Town Yetholm, if not Kirk Yetholm – at the house for irregular marriages[9] at Coldstream bridge.

They had a family of twelve, and in early days travelled the countryside selling earthenware. They camped on loanings and near woods, where they could obtain wood for their fires and game to keep themselves sustained for the days ahead.

Sometimes, she would call at the houses of the gentry. On one such occasion, she visited Lady Waterford at Ford Castle, and joined in the dancing. She did not recognise the music

---

[9] On the Scottish side of the Coldstream bridge - the Borders' equivalent of Gretna Green.

being played, and asked if the pianist could not play *Cuddle the Butler* or some well-known piece.

In 1866, she was visited by George Borrow[10], the great authority on Gypsies, who had travelled throughout Europe in his quest for knowledge of the life and language of the Gypsies.

In the course of his interview with Queen Esther, it appeared that she knew not more than 300 Gypsy words, some of which were not pure Gypsy words. Borrow said that she did not know much Gypsy, and used Cant and Gaelic terms. However, she possessed several words which are unknown to the English Romany, but are of the true Gypsy order.

Esther enjoyed receiving visitors, among them being Lady John Scott, who wrote *Annie Laurie* and other poetical pieces, some set to music. It was said that Lady John was connected with the Wauchope family of Niddrie, who were the lairds of Town Yetholm.

Esther occupied the small cottage now known as the Palace, which was probably built for her, as her sister Helen still occupied the old Palace. The one room, which was small, acted as a sort of living-room and bedroom. One lady whose parents occupied the palace in 1904 told me the children lay four to a bed, and a table was cut out specially to fit into the window.

Esther had special treasures, including a pistol which hung from the ceiling and a sword found on Flodden Field, as well as a sword of state, which was reputed to have been taken from an excise man in a skirmish. She also had a tin crown, which was the most precious of her possessions. When asked why her subjects did not subscribe towards a more elaborate and

---

[10] Author of *The Zincali: Gypsies of Spain* (1841) and *The Romany Rye* (1903).

expensive crown, she replied that a tin crown suited the purpose as well as a gold one would have done.

She once loaned the crown and a sword to the Hawick Archaeological Society for an exhibition held there in 1866. The crown was badly damaged and had to be repaired. The sword was left lying in Hawick for some months, and required cleaning. This obliterated the date impressed on the blade, which was supposed to be 332!

A visitor to Queen Esther at Kirk Yetholm in 1883 received a description of Yetholm as being 'sae mingle-mangle that one might think it was built on a dark nicht, or sawn on a windy one'.

By this time it was considered that the parish had lost much of its quaintness, and most of the old thatched cottages in Tinkers' Row, which were built with their gable ends to the Green, have had new ones built in their place.

In conversation, Esther bemoaned the changes that had taken place, which had affected her subjects so disadvantageously. Although a strict observer of the law, she thought the police acts were severe, and it was difficult for Gypsies who had poached all their lives to change their ways.

Esther fell upon difficult times financially and applied for assistance to the Jedburgh Parochial Board, as her husband had come from the town. The information given to the Board stated that she possessed a pony and trap with which she used to wander the countryside selling her wares.

She had twelve children, eight of them married and in no position to support her, so the Board offered her a place in the county poorhouse. Esther refused, considering it improper that such an offer should be made to a descendant of the house of Faa.

Esther died in a house of her daughter's in Kelso called 'The Castle'[11], and was buried in Kirk Yetholm on Sunday 15th July. Large crowds followed the hearse out of Kelso, and some 1,500 mourners received the coffin for the burial at Kirk Yetholm, but there were thought to be only about 25 to 30 Gypsies among the mourners.

---

[11] In Horsemarket.

KING CHARLES FAA BLYTH (RUTHERFORD) II

Reign 1898 – 1902

Coronation of King Charles Faa Blyth, 1898

It was some 15 years before the crowning of Charles Faa Blyth (as he was crowned), the eldest son of Esther, on Whit Monday 1898. This was merely a scheme to attract visitors to the village.

Charles had been a rover all his days, being employed here and there on a six-monthly basis. He was employed on the building of the railways in the north of England, and on bridge-building in and around Alnwick. He worked on farms at the busy times of the year, but the Gypsy wandering instinct wasn't far away, as he eventually hawked his goods around the countryside before finally returning to Kirk Yetholm to run a lodging house at the foot of the Muggers Row.

It appeared that Charles was a man of stocky character and had a good appearance, although he could not read or write.

The crowning committee involved several people from the villages: Carrick Miller, the minister, Archie Gladstone, the blacksmith, who acted as crowner, George Mather, the headmaster, who acted as Secretary, along with farmer John Stenhouse of Kirk Yetholm. The Committee were dressed up in the oddest costumes, which had been hired from a theatrical company in Glasgow. Among those leading the procession on horseback was John Stenhouse, and my grandfather, James Martin, a farmer in Town Yetholm.

It was estimated that between 10–15,000 people attended the crowning, which took place on Monday 30th May. The *Kelso Chronicle* gave a full description of the proceedings of the day.

'The royal carriage left 'The Palace', drawn by six gaily-caparisoned donkeys, yoked tandem fashion. […] The appearance of the royal carriage caused quite a stir, and there was great cheering and waving of hats, handkerchiefs, etc. […] The King-elect, who was accompanied by the Queen consort, had a tremendous reception, and, now the cynosure of all eyes, he, while duly appreciating the responsibilities of his position, was apparently in the best of spirits. Charlie, who was attired in a loose pale blue robe, faced with gold, whilst his wife, all smiles, was also specially robed, and wore on the head a plush circlet with gold facing to give it the appearance of a crown, very much resembles his mother in feature, and, despite his 70 years, he looked 'every inch a king' when, stepping from the carriage to the platform and then on to a chair, he, with special reference no doubt to the protest, declared with emphasis – 'King I am, and King I intend to be.'

The protest was a letter which came from Queen Esther's father, David Blyth, and was read out in public:

'8 Salamander Street, Leith,
20th May 1898

'Sir – I humbly protest against the claim of Charles Rutherford to the estate and title of Gypsy King. He has no right to claim the title. The lawful heir is David Blyth, of Chirnside, my father, who wishes to put forward his claim. My grandfather was former heir, but he objected to the title at the time, and handed it over to the late Queen Esther Faa Blyth. My father, David Blyth, and his cousin Charles, of Tweedmouth, have expressed their willingness to go to Yetholm and claim their right. Trusting you will kindly give this matter your best attention, and oblige,

Yours truly,
William Blyth'

However, David Blyth did not come forward to enforce his claim, and the ceremony went ahead as planned:

'The crown, the gift of Mr. Watt, and which had been specially made in London, was of brass, and was studded here and there with imitation jewels. Brought in when the Archbishop made his appearance, it rested on a cushion in the centre of the table, and at the proper time it was handed by Mr. Mather to the Archbishop [Archie Gladstone the blacksmith], who forthwith crowned Charlie as 'King Charles the Second'; his grandfather, the father of Queen Esther, was 'King Charles the First'.

'Charlie shrugged his shoulders and smiled broadly when the crown was placed on his head, and the crowd meanwhile cheered lustily. […] The Lord Chancellor [Watt the grocer] then, in impressive manner, read the following speech for the King.

'I am commanded by His Majesty the King of the Yetholm Gypsies to thank his loyal subjects for the great honour conferred on him this day, and to say that it will be his earnest endeavour to rule his people wisely and well. He trusts that his subjects of the royal villages of Town and Kirk Yetholm will live in peace and prosperity under his sway.' [12]

---

[12] *Kelso Chronicle*, 3rd June 1898.

Coronation of King Charles Faa Blyth II, attended by (from left) Robert Herbert, Archie Gladstone the blacksmith, Rev. Carrick Miller, Archie Watt the grocer and Dan Herbert

Coronation Procession of King Charles Faa Blyth, Town Yetholm, 1898

Crowds attending the coronation of King Charles Faa Blyth on the Green at Kirk Yetholm, 1898

King Charles Faa Blyth II

PRINCE ROBERT

uncrowned

It was suggested that Charles II's younger brother, Robert, might be elected King, but he was a man of poor character, being continually in trouble with the law.

He would sell wild rhubarb on the pretence it was good garden rhubarb, and sold glasses without glass in them to old ladies. He went to the minister of Makerston to sell a salmon which had been caught illegally, and asked 10/- for the fish. The sum was paid, and shortly after Robert returned to tell the minister the water bailiff was on his track, and the minister had better give him the fish back, since being in possession of illegally caught fish was a crime. The fish was handed back, but Robert kept the 10/-.

Lady John Scott had an interest in him, and when she arrived from London to stay in the Cross Keys Hotel in Kelso, Robert would arrive and be escorted to Hume the Tailors to have a good tweed suit made. The day before she returned to London, Robert would parade up and down adorned with the new suit, much to the pleasure and approval of Lady John Scott. She wasn't long onto the train to return to London when Robert had the suit sold to obtain money for drink.

When Lady John died, Robert accosted the hearse near Gordon for a lift to the funeral. At Spottiswoode, he lay in the back, to arrive at the home of the deceased.

The Young family of Kirk Yetholm near the old school (now the hostel), c. 1906

FOOD

The Gypsies' method of cooking a hen was to dig a hole in the ground and get a fire going. Take the hen unplucked, wrap it with straw, pat damp earth around it and place it in the fire. After a time, it would be considered cooked, the clay wrapping and feathers would fall off, and the chicken would be ready for eating.

In *Guy Mannering*, Sir Walter Scott describes how Meg Merrilees cooks her potage:

'Meg, in the meanwhile, went to a great black cauldron that was boiling on a fire on the floor, and lifting the lid, an odour was diffused through the vault, which, if the vapours of a witch's cauldron could in aught be trusted, promised better things than the hell-broth which such vessels are usually supposed to contain.

'It was in fact the savour of a goodly stew; composed of fowls, hares, partridges, and moorgame, boiled with potatoes, onions and leeks, and from the size of the cauldron, appeared to be prepared for half a dozen people at least. [...]

' "Aweel, eat your fill; but an ye kenn'd how it was gotten, ye maybe wadna like it sae weel. There's been mony a moonlight watch to bring a that trade thegither", continued Meg, – "the folk that are to eat that dinner thought little o' your game-laws."'[13]

It is interesting to observe that at the height of Gypsydom, the daughters in a family were married strictly according to age. The eldest was married first, and so on, and the youngest was the last to marry. Usually they were all married by the time they were 20, if marriageable. There were few marriages outside the tribe in early years, and those who did usually adopted the Gypsy way of life.

Divorce took the form of the parting couple walking down each side of a horse which had been sacrificed for the occasion. The husband repeated three times 'I divorce thee', and each made their own way in life, the man probably to take another wife, but the woman could not marry again. There do not appear to have been many divorces in Kirk Yetholm, as there was never any shortage of horses.

Most of the Gypsies were buried in the kirk yard in the village, and the clothes of the dead were burned. It was unlucky for anyone to wear them, as it would shorten their lives.

The Gypsies were superstitious and were strongly influenced by the senior females or 'surs' in the tribe. The Gypsies were about to leave for Mellerstain Entries one spring, when an old female dreamt that she had seen a hearse drawn by six headless black horses, and thought it to be a bad omen. So that year, that family did not visit Mellerstain.

Well over 100 years ago, the Duke of Roxburgh was travelling between Selkirk and St. Boswells and accidentally knocked

---

[13] Sir Walter Scott. *Guy Mannering*. London: Dent. 1906.

down a Gypsy child. The mother put a curse on the Duke, saying that the Dukes of Roxburgh would not live to see their sons' 21st birthday; for three generations, the Dukes have not lived until their sons' 21st.

The present Duke informed me that he had been to see a Gypsy medium a number of years ago, who informed him that the Gypsies no longer had a curse on the Duke of Roxburgh, which is true, as the Duke's eldest son is now over 21.

FIGHTING

There were a number of occasions when the Gypsies fought, mostly amongst themselves.

In 1677, the Faas and the Shaws from Dumfriesshire were returning from Haddington and near Romanno Bridge in Peeblesshire. They started to divide the spoils of their excursion when a dispute ensued. This ended up in a fight in which two of the Faas were killed. In the spring of the following year, four of the Shaws were hung on the Boroughmuir for causing these deaths. In Penicuik, a dovecote was erected on the spot where the fray took place; and to commemorate the battle, the following inscription was put upon the lintel of the door:

> *'The field of Gypsy blood which here you see,*
> *A shelter for the harmless dove shall be'.*

In 1772, at Lowrie's Den, an inn at the foot of Soutra Hill on the Lauder side, a murder took place in which Chas Anderson was struck down by Robert Keith. While his brother, William, held Anderson, Robert Keith fled, but was captured by country folk and Sir Walter Scott's father, who was among the pursuers. Keith was executed at Jedburgh on 24th November 1772.

In 1720, two Gypsy families arrived up in Ettrick in the area of Stobscleuch and Cossarhill, and were entertained by a young lad who played the fiddle and the pipes. This lad was attracted to a female in the other tribe, but her brother took exception to his advances.

A fight ensued, but the musician, losing courage, took refuge in the farmhouse at Cossarhill, where he was eventually caught by the antagonist and run through with a dagger. The Gypsy families arrived with a horse and took the dead Gypsy away to be buried at Stobscleuch, where his grave is marked by two large stones. No notice was taken of this event by the local authorities, since it was an occasion when the Gypsies were beholden to their own tribal laws.

In 1730, there was another fight at Hawick between the Yetholmites and those from Lochmaben, over a woman who had conferred her favours on a man from each disputing tribe. Two Gypsies died from their wounds, and several were taken to Jedburgh Jail.[14]

In 1773, there was a fight in Hawick known as the Battle of Hawick Brig, fought between the Kennedys of Lochmaben and the Taits from Yetholm. It would appear that the Kennedys were infiltrating into the area, which belonged to the Kirk Yetholm tribe.

The Gypsies had bludgeons, and some of the Taits carried cutlasses and similar weapons, which caused severe wounds to

---

[14] Details of the incident are described in Wilson's *History of Hawick*.

the Lochmaben tribe. Alexander Kennedy defended himself on a narrow bridge over the Teviot, and received a goodly supply of cudgels from the Hawick people with which to defend himself. The fight ceased when a party of constables marched the Taits off to prison, but no further action was taken, as there were no deaths.

There were other reported cases of fights and murders in which some of the murderers got off and others were despatched into the world beyond by the 'waefu wuddie'!

LANGUAGE

The Scottish Gypsies did everything possible to conceal that they had a language of their own. It appears that when they were asked about their speech, they exhibited an extraordinary degree of fear, caution and reluctance to admit they had a language of their own.

However, a certain number of words became known to non-Gypsies, some of which were genuine Gypsy words, others being Cant words. Among the Gypsy words in common use in Kirk Yetholm were:

bari	good
calshies	trousers
cashti	stick
chutli	pipe
chore	steal
deek	look
gadgie	man
guy	horse

jougal	dog
keir	house
lowie	money
manushi	woman
moey	mouth
peerie	foot
yak	eye
yarrie	egg

As mentioned earlier, Queen Esther knew only 300 Gypsy words. Some were pure Romany, but many were Cant or Fly[15] language words.

There was a story told that old David Blyth was dying and the minister was sent for. He said:

'David, I've told you all about God and the Devil. You're not frightened to go and meet your maker, are you?'

'No, I'm not frightened to meet my maker. It's yon other gadgie A'm feart o.'

---

[15] Described in detail in Joseph Lucas, *The Yetholm Gypsies*. Kelso: Rutherfurd & Craig, 1882.

RELIGION

It has been stated that the Gypsies had no religion. An intelligent Gypsy from Tweeddale was asked what religion his forefathers professed, and his answer was that 'the Gypsies had no religious sentiments at all; that they worshipped no sort of thing whatsoever'.

It was the influence of the Rev. John Baird which influenced the Kirk Yetholm Gypsies to adopt the Christian religion.

REV. JOHN BAIRD

Rev. John Baird became the minister of the kirk at Kirk Yetholm in the spring of 1829.

The manse was almost uninhabitable, the church was damp and thatched, and the only communication between the two villages was a narrow wooden bridge, which was swept away a few times a year.

The manse was enlarged and repaired, and the minister cultivated land running down towards the haugh and planted trees there. The old thatched kirk was pulled down and an enlarged, well-built one erected in its place. A stone-built bridge of three arches, wide enough for carts and carriages, was built to replace the wooden bridge between the two villages, and an embankment built along the road towards Kirk Yetholm to keep the flood in check.

Meanwhile, Mr. Baird was deeply aware of his responsibilities as minister of the parish – primarily, to influence the Gypsies to adopt the Christian way of life, by abandoning their wandering habits, staying at home, and taking work similar to the non-Gypsy residents of the village.

George Borrow said that the Gypsies have no system of religious beliefs, and are quite indifferent to all religious subjects. A writer in *Chambers's Miscellany* says that in England and Scotland, the Gypsies appear to exhibit the same carelessness regarding religion as their Spanish brethren; they seem, however, to be more alive to superstitious impressions. They apply to the clergyman of the parish where they take up their headquarters to have their children baptised, because they think it unlucky to have an unchristened child in the family.

Mr. Baird came to the conclusion that 'persons acquainted with the Gypsy only from books of imagination are led to connect something romantic and interesting with his character and manner of life. Had they a little personal acquaintance with the individuals themselves, the romantic sort of interest they feel in their condition would suffer very large abatement.

'There is, in fact, nothing romantic about the Gypsy but his free, roaming independent life – the sky his canopy, the cold earth his bed – having no master to restrain him, free to go hither and thither as his inclination leads him, changing his abode or encampment with almost every day he lives, a stranger to care, regardless of all weather and hardships, living above the law, or in defiance of it.

'We find on better acquaintance, that in general they are a set of idle, worthless, unprofitable, deceitful and dishonest vagabonds, with very few redeeming qualities. They hate all work; even the trades and occupations they follow are but an excuse for idleness. They will rather want than work, and steal rather than want.'[16]

Such was the odd people amongst whom Mr. Baird's lot was cast. His intention was to do everything possible to have the children remain at home and be educated, and attend the Sunday School and kirk on Sundays.

A committee was formed and a plan drawn up:

1. When the parents were from home – usually nine to twelve months of the year – the children were to be educated in the school specially built for them and non-Gypsy children. The Gypsy children were to be boarded in families in the village or to stay in their own homes with a suitable person to look after them.
2. When the children left school, the boys would be apprenticed to a trade, such as a joiner or bricklayer, or work on the farms. The girls would obtain work as servants in the big houses, where they would

---
[16] Source unclear.

receive keep and shelter and not much more.

3. The parents would be enticed to cease their wandering ways and obtain work and stay at home. This would mean that they would look after their own children. There were difficulties, among them being:

(a) The dislike generally entertained to the race, the jealousy of non-Gypsies of so much attention being paid to such worthless characters, and the want of encouragement, sympathy and co-operation from those who might be expected to help and whose assistance would be useful.

(b) Connected with the dislike of the race, the difficulty of getting children accommodated when left at home, or getting people to supervise. One Gypsy mother said she would leave her two daughters, but who would look after them? The minister said that when she called at the manse the next day, he would let her know. That day, the minister went round every non-Gypsy house in Kirk Yetholm asking for accommodation for the girls, but no one would take them. The next day, when the Gypsy mother called at the manse to enquire about her two daughters, the minister said that they would stay at the manse, and

(c) The attitude of the Gypsy parents, being greedy and unreasonable, deceitful and jealous of each other, and the evil habits of the children and the slow progress in correcting them.

(d) The dislike of the non-Gypsy children, who didn't like to sit beside them or associate with them.

In 1843, a new and commodious schoolhouse was built in Kirk Yetholm, which is now the youth hostel. A teacher well qualified for his duties was appointed.

It was a difficult undertaking, with upwards of 100 pupils attending, comprising both Gypsy and non-Gypsy children. Progress was initially slow, but gradually the Gypsy children were as well behaved as the non-Gypsy children.

The teacher's salary was not great, and in the autumn he had to take a harvesting job to augment his income. The holidays were decided when the corn was ready for reaping. The country children would bring in a few ripe ears of corn and present them to the teacher, saying 'teacher, you'll have to take the holidays – the corn's ready'.

The second part of the plan was to have the Gypsy parents stay at home and obtain work locally, which initially was unsuccessful.

However, when the hawking law was enforced and camping

on the roadsides was banned, more Gypsies started to stay at home.

The costs of running the school were extremely important. If the children were boarded out, the cost could be 2/- to 2/6 per week. If the children stayed in their own homes, the cost would be 1/6 per week on average. They were also given meals, which amounted to £35 per year.

The schoolmaster's wages were 10/- per year for each child. With over 100 children attending school, that amounted to £50 to £60 per year as a salary. The committee was responsible for paying this salary, and the cost of books for the children also had to be met. The committee depended on grants and donations from local people, and they were hard pushed at times to 'balance the books'.

In 1861, there was a religious revival, and many of the Gypsies attended kirk regularly. Unfortunately, at the height of this good work, when the labours of the minister were coming to fruition, Mr. Baird died.

In 1872, the compulsory education act was passed, which eliminated the private costs of running this school.

At this time, there was a move for the Gypsies to settle down and move to other Border towns, where they sold earthenware, china, etc.

With the coming of the industrial revolution, items which the Gypsies sold could be made much cheaper.

FAIRS

St. James' Fair, Kelso Square, 1886

A great attraction to country folk was the annual fair. In Yetholm and Kirk Yetholm, two fairs were held each year, and at least one was held on Staerough, known as the Rough Hogg Fair. Little is known about what else took place at these fairs, except that there was racing over 200 yards from the Stank Brig in 1870.

A great attraction in the Borders was St. Boswells Fair, held on 18th July in each year. Initially, this was largely a sheep and cattle fair, but it extended to a fair selling linen, farm produce and goods of all descriptions, including ironmongery and pottery, as well as tinkers, fortune-telling and horse trading, especially by the Gypsies.

People from all parts of the Borders attended, with busloads even coming from Edinburgh. The fair dated from as far back as 1621. At one time, it was held in Maxton Haugh, but because of floods it was transferred to the Green, its permanent home.

Originally it was a seven-day event, but in the early 19th century it was restricted to one day.

This was a great event for the Gypsies, who travelled from as far afield as Yorkshire. These visitors did not mix with the local Gypsies and camped away from each other. In the early days before caravans, there were carts turned upside down with straw for the bed and a tarpaulin cover reaching to the ground for a night's shelter. Fires were lit at the front of each shelter for cooking, and near at hand was an ample supply of firewood.

The dues from the fair were paid to the Duke of Buccleuch and amounted generally to £40. A horse sold at around 2/-, a sheep at around eight pence.

There was much to attract the visitors, who were there to buy and be entertained; there were cakes, sweets, hobby horses, coconut shies, shooting galleries, boxing booths and fortune telling, where young maidens queued to be told their fortune.

There was a great deal of stealing by the Gypsies, especially the children. A story is told of one farmer's wife attending the fair and having her purse stolen. She quickly sought out a Gypsy mother, demanding the return of her purse. The Gypsy invited the farmer's wife into her tent to look into the basket to see if her purse was there.

'There it is,' said the farmer's wife.

'Now count your money to see if it is all there.'

'Yes, it is.'

'Now isn't it grand to deal with good honest folk?' replied the Gypsy.

GYPSY CHARACTERS
MADGE GORDON

Madge Gordon was the granddaughter of Jean Gordon, and Sir Walter Scott remembers her when she called at Abbotsford. She was married to a Young – one of the chief families in the Gypsy race – but as Madge Gordon, her striking personality is still remembered on the Border, as described in Jean Lang's *North and South of Tweed*.

'She was a remarkable personage, of a very commanding presence and high stature, being nearly six feet high. She had a large aquiline nose, penetrating eyes even in her old age, bushy hair that hung around her shoulders from beneath a Gypsy bonnet of straw, a short cloak of a peculiar fashion, and a long staff nearly as tall as herself […] When she spoke vehemently (for she made loud complaints), she used to strike her staff upon the floor, and throw herself into an attitude which it was impossible to regard with indifference. She used to say that she could bring, from the remotest parts of the island, friends to revenge her quarrel, while she sat motionless in her cottage; and she frequently boasted that there was a time when she was of still more considerable importance, for there were at her wedding fifty saddled asses, and unsaddled asses without number.'

'Possibly Madge's boast of the friends who would come to revenge her quarrel had something to do with a pardon obtained for two of her kinsmen – Gordons both – convicted of murder. This was to the exasperation of that uncompromising old prop of the law, Lord Braxfield, prototype of Weir of Hermiston.

'"It's hard we cannae get a scoonrel hangit," he growled, "however richly he deserves it, without some fule o' a wumman interferin' wi' the job."

'It is not many years since there died one whose account of a race between him and Madge Gordon, her elf locks and red cloak flying behind her, and her long staff in her hand, was one well worth listening to.

'Young Andrew Currie, of Howford, up Ettrick, was apprenticed to a wheelwright at Denholm, and on a lonely road between Denholm and Ettrick Water he saw the old Gypsy legging it along for all she was worth. He was on the high road, she on a track above it, but in a few hundred yards the roads converged, and into the boy's impish mind there came the notion that he would like to try a walking race with the old woman, without her consent or knowledge. That was, however, a scheme easier to think of than to carry out. Madge Gordon soon became aware that a boy with eyes as dark and Gypsy-like as those of any of her own brood was taking the unpardonable liberty of racing with her on the public highway. She shouted to him, and he responded with a boyish jeer. And then the fun began. Madge

57

ran, and the boy ran, and behind Madge came an unexpected reinforcement of a sturdy young Gypsy with an ass laden with crockery. The boy, nearly winded, pounded along the high road. Could he win past the spot where the upper path joined the lower, there was still hope for him. But he had not calculated on the pace of that fearsome old woman with muscles and sinews of steel. It was like a nightmare. He could run no more, and when a pair of brawny brown hands laid hold on him from behind, he gave himself up for lost. But Madge Gordon was not one to hang even a dog without fair trial.

"'In the first place, whae are ye? And where do ye come frae?" she demanded.

"'Well then, gudewife, I have come from Denholm," said the boy.

"'And whae do ye belong to at Denholm? I ken everybody there; there's baith gude and bad in't, frae auld Duncan to Sergeant Houston. Tell me at aince, whae are yere folk?"

"'Have patience, mistress," said Andrew Currie. "I only said I had come from Denholm. I have only stayed there since last Whitsunday, and I wish to goodness I had never seen it. My native place is in Ettrick, about the Brig-end."

"'Weel, I ken the Brig-end and everybody in't as weel as I ken Denholm, and whae has the misfortune to own ye there? Be quick, and nane o' yere dodging wi' me, for I'll hae't oot o' ye, and something else, afore I pairt wi' ye."

"'Well, well, mistress, ye have a perfect right, for you're the victor, and can impose what terms you like on me. I was born at Howford, and I am Andrew Currie, the son, and the oldest one, of William Currie, who again was the son –" Amazing was the effect of this intelligence upon Madge Gordon.

'"What's that ye say, younker?" she asked, and placed her basket down on the road. "Say nae mair, younker; I ken yer forebears baith by faither's and mother's side far better than ye do yersel', and the Lord be thankit that I ken whae ye are, for, tae be plain wi' ye, I intended to hae gien you a thrashing that ye wad hae minded to the langest day o' yere life; but syne ye're the grandson o' twae gude men that aince did me and mine a gude turn, saved me and my weans frae starvation i' the dear years – that, of coorse, alters the case entirely, and I freely forgie ye on their account yere impudent trick on an auld wife. Weel, weel, eneuch said; I see ye're sorry for't, and ye wadna be yer gude-hairted faither's bairn if ye wasna'. But here's Matthew, ma son, an' I see he has been knottin' his whup for yere back; but fearna', he sall ne'er lay a finger on ye."

'Up came the scowling Matthew, whip upraised, to avenge the insulted dignity of her who was practically queen of the Yetholm Gypsies, but Madge stepped between him and the apprehensive Andrew.

'"Haud yere hand, Matthew," she said. "It was his grandfaither that saved your life when ye was a suckin' bairn, and fed and clothed yere faither and mither at Brownmuir. You and him will stop and crack here till I gae doon and hawk the herd's hoose; syne I want to hae a crack wi' him as far as we gang thegither, and that wull be to Hartwoodmyres, I'm thinkin', sae be freends."

'"Freends," too, did the sturdy Gypsy and the boy speedily become, the subject of dogs proving a strong bond of union.

"'My mither's very muckle respeckit," proudly spoke Matthew Young, "and sae was her mither, Eppie Faa, amang oor folk, and even by mony o' the gentry. The Shirra, when he was at Ashiestiel, and huz camped aboot Thornilee, wud hae grannie crackin' wi' him for hoors aboot auld-warld things, and weel read she was, in a' kind o' lair and spaein'. They tell me he made a buik aboot her. Weel, I dinna ken what it was a' aboot, or what they ca'ed the buik; ma mither will likely ken; but I ken this, that he tauld her never to gang by Abbotsford wi'oot ca'ing in and getting a drink o' yill, and a feed for the yaud. He is awfu' gude, is the Shirra, to huz puir bodies."

'When Madge Gordon returned from a successful interview with the herd's wife, half a crown in pocket, the cracks at once began, and young Currie was given many an item in the history of his own family of which he had until then been in ignorance.

"'What was the good turn you said my grandfather did to you?" he asked.

"'Aweel, I'll tell ye aboot that," said the Gypsy. "Afore ye was born, there was a famine in the land, and I daursay mony ane perished o' want that winter, what wi' cauld and what wi' hunger, and this near happened to huz – that is, to faither and mither, mysel', and three bairns – till hunger drave us to tak means to save oor lives, and for that we was mairched up to Selkirk Cross, wi' oor bits o' cuddies, and my auld faither, fair gane wi' the trouble that ended his days, harled through the snaw wi' the handcuffs on him, to the jail; and I had to stand at the Cross wi' my greetin' bairns till oor bits o' gudes was sell't to pay expense o' poindin'. I believe I had it on my lips to invoke a fearfu' curse on some that shall be nameless, when auld John Lang steppit up to me and says kindly, like a ministerin' angel, 'Ma gude woman, ye're at liberty to gang awa wi' yere gudes; a freend has paid the fine for ye, and here's five shillings to get some meat for yersel' and bairns; after that, ye wull get lodging at Mr. Curror's, Brownmuir.' Afore this my heart was steeled, but at the kind words I fairly lost the field and grat till I thocht it wad break, and I saw the gude-hearted auld man turn his back and tak oot his pocket-naipkin to dicht his een. I invoked a blessing on him and his, and on yere faither's faither that kept us, and fed us, and set us a' gain' again, and that blessing will be felt for time to come; I dinna say in this generation, but tent ma words, Providence wull yet reward that gude deed. I hae aye ta'en a kind interest in baith the families, and keepit masel' acquent, through my cousin Rachael at the foot o' the Kirkwynd, o' the weelfare o' their bonny family."

'Thus did Madge Gordon shorten for her boy companion that walk to Hartwoodmyres. She was, he knew, a notable spaewife, and yet it was said that her powers of divination were far inferior to those of her grandmother and even those of Eppie, her mother, and so when she spoke to him of his uncle, John Lang, ensign of the 94th, who was shot as he carried his flag on to the ramparts of Badajos on the night that the town was taken, the boy felt overawed.

'"I was very wae when that young lad gaed sodgering to Spain," she said, "but mair by token they used to come aboot the camp to get their fortunes spaed with my mither, for she was wonderfu' at the glamoury; and I mind aince, when we were campit on Bullsheugh Brae, and i' the Sunday efternoon yere grandfaither and his wife, Jean Sibbald, and a' the young folk, cam oot for their walk, and I said to my mither, 'Did ye ever see sic a bonny family?' 'Sae they are, sae they are,' says she, 'but there's dule, dule[17] for the best and bonniest o' them a'. I didna' ken what she meant, and didna' tak muckle heed at the time, but I often thocht o't after when the young sodger was shot through the heid."

'Andrew Currie lived to be an old man and a fine sculptor; one may see his *Ettrick Shepherd* at St. Mary's Loch, his *Mungo Park* in Selkirk, his *Edie Ochiltree* and others on the Scott Monument in Edinburgh, and other good work in other parts of Scotland. But long ere his race was run, Madge Gordon's wandering ceased. A degenerate, mongrel, 'mugger' horde has taken the place of the old Gypsy race, and the glories of Yetholm have passed away.' [18]

---

[17] Grief.
[18] Jean Lang. *North and South of Tweed*. London: T.C. & E.C. Jack, 1913.

JOCK BLYTHE
1869 – 1947

Jock Blythe thatching the old sweetie shop, Town Yetholm

Jock was born in Kirk Yetholm in 1869 and died in 1947. He stayed in the small cottage at the top of the hill going into Kirk Yetholm from Town Yetholm, opposite the Kirk. He was one of the last Gypsies who had adopted the village way of life. He thatched the roofs of the straw houses, and at times worked as a labourer. He was also the gravedigger in the kirk yard adjacent to his cottage.

One night there was a knock at the door, and this old Gypsy widow invited Jock to go over to the kirkyard and said to Jock:

'Jock, when A die A want to be buried in that bit o' ground aback o' the wa in that nice bielded bit.'

'Mary, ye'll have tae lie where your man Andra lies. What's folk gannie think?'

'Jock, if ye dinnae bury me a back o' the dyke A'll haunt you all your days.'

'Mary, as sure as anything ye'll get buried a back o' the dyke'.

When Mary died, her son came to Jock the gravedigger, to make arrangements for the funeral.

'Ma mother will get buried just where my father's buried, of course.'

'No, no son – your mother had a bit o' ground a back o' the dyke in a nice bielded bit, as she said, and that's where she's getting buried.'

After a long discussion, Jock said: 'Well, I'll bury your mother beside your father, but if she haunts me yin night, up she comes'.

Jock was also a chimney sweep, and often looked a darkish shade of black when about his business. He was carrying a bag of soot out of a house one day when the dog of the house objected and nipped him on the leg. The lady of the house was a bit upset and gave Jock a dram to soothe his nerves. The husband suggested in through the kitchen that she also should have a wee drappie, and when Jock heard the clinking of glasses, he shouted, 'if that's another yin for me, nae water in it mind'.

Jock was brought up in the Gypsy tradition, 'whenever ye gan oot, aye come back wi something'.

Jock and his accomplice, Bobby Laidlaw, once went poaching salmon on the Kale up at Morebattle, and on the return journey, carrying a sack of salmon, got caught by a severe snowstorm. They took shelter in the cart shed at Primside, and Bobby noticed Jock reaching up to the jeests,[19] which were a bit low. Bobby noticed that the hens were roosting there, and Jock was feeling each hen.

'What are ye daen, Jock?'

'Well A'm no gannae take a lean yin.'

Jock carried out the duties of 'biddin the funerals' – an advice to householders in the village that someone in the village had died, and they were invited to attend the funeral on a certain day and time. I have not heard of this practice in any other village. It ceased in about 1945.

Jock had a wonderful sense of humour. During the First World War, he came into the house and said, 'there was a German Zeppelin came low over me as I walked down the haugh. I could see the pilot looking down, and he shouted to me 'is it a soft landing in the meadow, Blythe?'

Jock said that he had once been digging a grave and had picked up a string of beads, which he had put in his pocket. On returning home he put them on a bedside table but was woken up through the night by them shaking. He got up and went to the kirkyard and buried them, as he wasn't going to be bothered with them for the rest of his life.

Jock would say 'in the wonderful summer days lang syne, efter ma denner A would go and lie doon a back o' a heid stane. Man, it's a grand thing when ye can rise up frae a back o' a heidstane. A wus lyin there yin day when A heard the kirk

---

[19] Joists.

65

gates opening. A lifted my heid onto my hands and said 'It's a grand day, ladies'.

'Oh, yes, it is. We were wanting to have a look around the churchyard. Is there anything to pay?'

'No, no unless you're bidin!'

Jock held the important position of being the minister's man. Well do I remember him dressed up in his frock coat and striped trousers, carrying the big Ha' bible, ascending the pulpit and placing the bible on the lectern. He would return up the kirk and seek the minister, who followed him, and Jock would step aside for the minister to enter the pulpit for Jock to follow and lock him in.

The last minister that Jock served under, Mr. McFadden, had been there about a year when his brother visited the kirk one Sunday. He asked Jock how things were going:

'Oh, very weel, very weel. What he disnae ken A tell him, and what A dinnae ken he tells me.'

One of the ministers that Jock served under said to him one day: 'John, you know so much about the church that if I were unable to take the service, I'm sure you could take it.'

'Weel, minister, I'll tell you this much: A wud fill the Kirk, for everybody wud come to hear Jock Blythe preaching.'

Jock served under five ministers.

JOHN TAIT
(STOVIE JOCK)
1855 – 1924

Stovie Jock was so called for his great love of stovie tatties. He would call at a row of houses on the farm when out selling his wares, and ask a household for twae or three tatties, then he would beg a pickle pig belly fat, and he was nearly there for a feast.

Jock, a native of Kirk Yetholm and Gypsy bred, had the reputation of being a wild man in his younger days, repeatedly falling foul of the law through poaching. At a trial held for murder, it was stated that Jock and his brother-in-law, Will Blyth, set out to ferret rabbits on Kilham farm in Northumberland in November 1880.

According to the court transcripts, as the two men were digging, the shepherd John Taylor came along and enquired what they were up to. On receiving the reply 'getting a bit rabbit', the shepherd said that it was a pity, as someone had paid the farmer to 'catch' the rabbits on the place. The shepherd asked Blyth what he was howkin with, and Blyth replied: 'I'll knock your head with it'. In Taylor's account, 'Blyth then spat in my face. I did not charge the men with stealing the rabbits; I endeavoured to stop them from taking them. They never used any violence towards me with the exception of spitting in my face.'

Thomas Allan stated that he was a gamekeeper in the employment of Mr. Selby at Pawston. On the 15th November, he was on his rounds, and met Thomas Henry Scott, police constable, on the road between Kilham and Yetholm. 'The deceased communicated something to me and I went back with him to Coldmouth Gate Field. It is a gate across the highway and encloses part of the moorland. There is only one wall at that point.'

Tait and Blyth came down the hill where Allan and PC Scott were standing at about 6 o'clock. They had a lot of rabbits coupled over their shoulders. PC Scott demanded the rabbits, which were taken off their backs by Scott and laid on the ground. They had about ten rabbits each. The policeman said that the rabbits were his property, as they had been unlawfully taken from another man's ground. The police constable then searched Tait, and said that there were two rabbits in his pockets.

Allan the gamekeeper said he searched Blyth and found a ferret in his pocket.

Polisman's Gate, scene of PC Scott's fatal injury in 1880

After the search, the prisoners picked up the rabbits and threw them over the wall, uttering words to the effect that they would rather die than give up the rabbits. They followed the rabbits over the wall and the policemen and gamekeeper Allan followed. They got over about ten or 20 yards from the gate on the Yetholm side.

The PC then gripped Tait by the collar and demanded the two rabbits. Tait shouted to Blyth 'Pick up a stane and fell the bastard!' Blyth picked up a stone and threw it at Scott's head. Allan says that although he did not see it make contact, it must have done as PC Scott stopped and fell, and put his hand up to the left side of his head after his helmet had fallen off.

In Allan's account, the ground at the spot where PC Scott was struck slopes down towards the dyke, and the constable called out 'I am killed'. He got up again and was going away between the burn and the wall towards Yetholm, when Tait followed him up, picked a stone off the wall, as much as he could hold, and threw it at Scott's head. The deceased staggered a little bit forward and fell into the burn.

After Tait had thrown the stone and the policeman had fallen into the syke, Tait was laying into him with a club, which the Gypsies usually carry with them.

Allan says he held Blyth by the right arm but let him go as Tait threw the stone at Scott's head. He ran to Scott in the ditch, but by this time he was insensible. He lifted his head out of the syke and laid it on the side of the bank.

Tait ran off a little bit and stood; he was coming a second time, flourishing his stick, swearing he would kill them both. Allan had a loaded gun with him and said: 'If you throw another stone or touch me with that stick I will put a hole through you'. Tait then went away, and Blyth had the rabbits picked up and they went off together.

Scott asked Allan to take him home as 'his head was in a jelly'. The gamekeeper got a cart at Shotton and took him to Pawston, where he got medical assistance.

Scott died of tetanus, directly due to injury to the brain apparently caused by stones.

Mr. Walton, acting for the defence, stated there was no evidence given to the jury in support of the major charge of murder, and the facts proved that the crime must be reduced to that of manslaughter.

There were no less than five contradictions in the statements made by Scott the deceased policeman and Allan the gamekeeper.

The jury retired for 20 minutes and returned with a verdict of manslaughter against both prisoners.

In passing sentence, his lordship said: 'John Tait, the jury have found you guilty of manslaughter. They have taken a most merciful view of your case – I think the worst case of manslaughter that has come under my notice. [...] You have been guilty on several occasions of offences against the law, including assault against the gamekeeper, Allan, for which you underwent twelve months' imprisonment.

'You have also given yourself up to poaching, which is sometimes looked upon as a very venial offence, but it is an offence that often leads to the most serious consequences, and especially when a person gives himself up to it is a man of evil passions, and does not hesitate at violence. You have had a very narrow escape for your life, but it is my duty to pass upon you the most serious sentence that I can for manslaughter, that is, penal servitude for life.

'William Blyth: your case is essentially different from the other [...] The sentence upon you is ten years' penal servitude.

'Tait, who is a dark, sullen-looking man, and stated to be a Gypsy, received his sentence unmoved, but with a severely crestfallen aspect; while Blyth, who had been much the more cheerful of the two men [...] made a movement with his hand to the judge and said 'Thank you' when his term of imprisonment was named.'[20]

---

[20] Trial transcripts from *Kelso Chronicle*, 3rd December 1880.

Jock served his 20 years in prison, and one day in January 1900 he disembarked from a train at Mindrum Station. My grandfather was carting coals from Mindrum to Yetholm and, seeing Jock, offered him a lift up to the village. Jock accepted and on the journey home, Jock related a few stories on prison life.

One was that when out for exercise with a few of the warders, he was so hungry that he slipped into a potato field and stole one or two potatoes, which he devoured in the raw state, being so hungry. When he got to the Stank corner near Yetholm, he jumped off the cart and waded the Bowmont, as he did not wish to walk through Yetholm.

Jock was born in 1851, and married Ellen Rutherford, daughter of Queen Esther, in 1878. They had only one of a family – a daughter, Beatrice. When Jock returned from prison he stayed on his own in a but-and-ben next to the Palace further up the 'raw'. His wife, Ellen, had moved to Kelso and stayed with her daughter, Beatrice.

He had in his later career only a house mate – his jougal[21], Mack. Mack would come out in the morning and give himself a shake; Jock would do similar, draw his hand down over his face and sniff the morning air, debating within himself where he should travel.

There was the pownie or cuddy, Jeannie, to be collected from the Common Land. One day as Jock was collecting the pownie, the hounds came through the land as Jock was riding home, when he received a torrent of abuse from the master of the hounds.

---

[21] Dog.

'You've come through the very place we were about to draw for the fox, and look at you, you old fool, riding on a donkey.'

In true Gypsy fashion, Jock replied: 'Ma man, never make a fool o' any man who rode on a donkey; oor Lord rode on a donkey.'

And might not the donkey, when it saw the blood horses, think of the words of GK Chesterton's poem to the donkey:

'Fools for I also had my hour, one fast fierce hour and sweet,
There was a shout about my ears and palms before my feet.'

Jock travelled the countryside selling his bits of wares with Jeannie, the cuddy, and Mack the jougal, the bread winner. He was especially welcomed by 'ootbye' folk as the bearer of news of 'gainins on' at local farms, and news from further afield which had a *News of the World* flavour.

From a distance, he would holler his imminent approach, and a place would be set for him at the table end to partake of the guid hame-made kale, made with stock from a bit of hill lamb and vegetables from the back garden. Guid wholesome fare.

One day in later years, as he was returning from selling at Morebattle, to ease the burden from Jeannie the cuddy as they climbed the hill, he dismounted from the cart. At that time, workers in a field adjacent to Primside Brae were having their afternoon break, when the steward, a young cocky individual, remarked 'Here comes auld Stovie Jock. I'll pull his leg, I'll renk[22] him.'

---
[22] Tease.

'Aye, Jock, that auld cuddy o' yours is getting guy hard up.'

'Aye, it is, ma man, and A canna get a replacement for the auld cuddy.'

'How is that, Jock?'

'Maist o the farmers are takin them as stewards!'

Jock had a great sense of humour.

There was one occasion when he met Admiral Oliver from the local estate of Lochside, and the Admiral remarked:

'Tait, I understand you keep donkeys, and I believe donkeys are very good at eating thistles. Now I have a field of thistles I can do nothing with. Would you bring out some of your donkeys to eat my thistles?'

'Yes, Admiral, I'll fairly do that.'

After a few weeks, the Admiral met Stovie Jock and said:

'Now look here, Tait – those donkeys of yours are not making one bit of impression on the thistles.'

'But gie them time admiral, gie them time. Wait till they eat a' the gress first'.

Jock spent odd days working at potato gathering, harvesting and threshing in the small farms around the village. When farmers had to help each other at threshing, inevitably additional helpers would be required, and Jock would be included in this category. Jock was always full of praise for the repast, complimenting the lady of the house that it was the best meal he had partaken since the last threshing.

During the First World War, and also the Second, there was a law against displaying a light in case German planes were attracted.

I remember my grannies telling us some 60 years ago that Stovie Jock was summoned to the court for this offence. The Procurator Fiscal called the first witness – the policeman, who stated:

'I was on duty in Kirk Yetholm on the night of 16th November 1916, when I noted a light some eight feet by six feet shining into the roadway, and charged the accused John Tait with this offence.'

The judge asked the accused what he had to say for himself.

'Well, my Lord, A never thought a ha'penny candle could give as muckle light.'

Jock was always treated to a bit of leg pulling, and on one occasion when he was ill and taken to his bed, he was paid a visit by the village blacksmith, Wullie Gled (William Gladstone), who was returning a farmer's horses to Kirk Yetholm after having it shod. After some time, the blacksmith said that he would have to rush home to have his 'denner', as the Cherrytree horses were due to be shod at one o'clock.

Jock told him to sit still a bit longer and if he didn't, Mack the dog would make sure he did.

'Watch him Mack,' said Jock, and as Mack approached with bared teeth, Wullie was firmly anchored to the chair. 'Jock, ye'll have to let me go. Ca' off the jougal.'

'Wullie Gled, you've renked me a the days o' your life. Jist bide still.'

Eventually, Wullie was allowed to go from his captivity, having only time for a walk round the table for denner before attending to the horses' feet.

Wullie told me that he was never so moved with any experience in his life as when Jock approached the smiddy door with Jeannie, his cuddy. Wullie said, 'Jock, A canna shoe the cuddy the day. A'm ower busy'.

'Am no wantin ye to shoe the cuddy, Wullie. I hear that your cuddy died yesterday. Ye can have the use o mine until ye get another.' Extreme gratitude from an unexpected quarter.

Many stories are told about Jock, one being that he came to fisticuffs with Charlie, the village scaffie[23], a most unlikely contender for a pugilistic title. On the day of the court case, Jock was chatting to a few of the worthies of Jedburgh outside the court, when Charlie passed by on his way to the hearing, and Jock remarked, 'stand back, ye Jethart fellas. Here's the fighting man o' Yetholm comin.'

It would appear that when Jock was reaching his end, admittance to his house could not be obtained because of Jock being bed-ridden and Mack the dog guarding the door. It is sad to report that the dog had to be shot to gain entry, so that Jock could be removed to Inch Home, Kelso, where he ended his days in 1924.

Jock was married to one of Queen Esther's daughters, Ellen, who died in 1924. Ellen nursed her mother, Queen Esther, in Kelso, until she died in 1883.

Jock and Ellen had one daughter only: Beatrice, born in 1879, who married William James Gilroy Scott in 1905. They had a daughter, Mary Eleanor Rutherford Tait, who married Robert Cairns of Hawick. In their family they had a daughter, Beatrice, who married Gerald Greengrass. Beatrice resides in

---

[23] Refuse collector.

Romford in the wintertime and in Hawick in the summertime. To be out of the beautiful Border country for the winter is just too long.

Her daughter, Janet, has a strong interest in the Gypsies, and her husband, son and daughter are delightful people. Janet is appreciative of the country and people she is descended from. Queen Esther was her great, great, great grandmother.

ANDREW BLYTHE

1851 - 1933

As a young Gypsy lad, Andrew was involved in an accident, which resulted in one of his arms being amputated. He attended Sunday School and kirk, and sang the old favourites *All People That on Earth*, *O God of Bethel* and *I to the Hills Will Lift my Eyes*.

One day, he took to the hills to seek his living, with sixpence in his pocket, and all his worldly goods in a knapsack, calling at shepherds' cottages on the English side of the Border, where he taught the children. He stayed a week or two with each family, depending on the number of children, and then moved on.

Eventually he stayed at Loungerknowe at Windyhaugh, near the source of the River Coquet, and taught children from the surrounding district reading, writing and arithmetic, and Bible lessons too, in a byre and then in a stable as there was no other accommodation. Eventually he was passed out as a teacher by the Northumberland Education Authority, a school was built and he taught there for 40 years.

But he returned each weekend to Kirk Yetholm, when he

came home to his folk. He came to where he worshipped and gave his services to the kirk, where he became the session clerk. There are not many reminders of the Gypsies' presence in Kirk Yetholm from past years, except the school (now the youth hostel), the Palace, and the annual local festival, when the principals are the Bari Gadgie and Manushi. There is also the written word, which will never die or fade away.

Stuart Smith gives the blessing to Bari Gadgie Murray Freeland-Cook and Bari Manushi Heather Stewart at the Stob Stane, 2003

Will Ogilvie, our Border poet, who visited Kirk Yetholm often, wrote a number of poems about the Gypsies, and I quote two verses from one:

'O tell me what the stars have told your quiet camps at night!
What letters on the dark unrolled your fires' red fingers write!
And tell my why the willows weep and what the larches croon
When their boughs are crossed with silver by the bonny harvest moon!

And tell me where the white roads lead that lure you on and on,
And why the days grow dark indeed when once your wheels are gone!
And tell me why I miss you so, and why my wild heart grieves
For you that come like buds in spring and go like autumn leaves!

But it is not only in spring and autumn, but the whole year round that Andrew Blythe is remembered. His life is commemorated in a stained glass window in Kirk Yetholm church. He exemplifies the changes in the Gypsies' way of life, eventually teaching children in a byre and a stable about our Lord, who was born in a stable.

It can be said of the Gypsies who stayed in Kirk Yetholm that, by saving a physical life in battle – that of the then Laird, Captain Bennet – they were introduced to a spiritual life. They were given the opportunity of entering and accepting the larger worldwide bond of brotherhood, that of the Christian Church.

Perhaps Andrew Blythe's appointment as a church elder, then Session Clerk, finally brings the Reverend John Baird's dream to fruition as a sign of the Gypsies' full acceptance in Kirk Yetholm.

Stained glass windows in Kirk Yetholm Church, with inscription in memory of Andrew Blythe

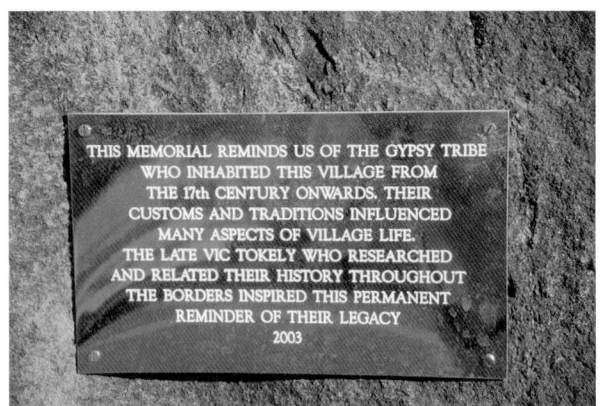

Plaque in memory of the Gypsies of Kirk Yetholm

*Tokely family members at the unveiling of the memorial stone,
Kirk Yetholm, 2003*

BIBLIOGRAPHY

Borrow, George. *The Zincali: Gypsies of Spain*. London: John Murray, 1841.

Borrow, George. *The Romany Rye*. London: John Murray, 1903.

Gordon, Anne. *Hearts Upon the Highway – Gypsies in South-East Scotland.* Galashiels: McQueen, 1980.

Keats, John. *Poetical Works.* Oxford: OUP, 1970.

Lang, Jean. *North and South of Tweed.* London: T C & E C Jack, 1913.

Lucas, Joseph. *The Yetholm Gypsies.* Kelso: Rutherfurd & Craig, 1882.

Murray, R. *The Gypsies of the Border.* Galashiels: T.F. Brockie, 1875.

Ogilvie, Will. *Saddle for a Throne.* Adelaide: R.M. Williams, 1852.

Scott, Walter. *Guy Mannering.* London: Dent. 1906.

Simson, Walter. *A History of the Gipsies*. London: Samson, Low, 1865.

Tokely, A V *The Kirk Yetholm Gypsies.* Borders Family History Society, 1996.

Whyte, Donald. *Scottish Gypsies and Other Travellers.* Blackwell, Alfreton: Robert Dawson, 2001.

Wilson, Robert. *A History of Hawick.* Hawick: 1841.

APPENDIX

JOHNNY FAA

The gypsies came to my Lord Cassilis' yett,
And O but they sang bonnie!
They sang sae sweet, and sae complete
That down came our fair ladie.

She came tripping down the stairs,
And all her maids before her;
As soon as they saw her weel-far'd face,
They coost their glamourie owre her.

She gave to them the good wheat bread,
And they gave her the ginger;
But she gave them a far better thing,
The gold ring off her finger.

'Will ye go with me, my hinny and my heart?
Will ye go with me, my dearie?
And I will swear, by the staff of my spear,
That your lord shall nae mair come near thee.'

'Sae take from me my silk manteel,
And bring to me a plaidie,
For I will travel the world owre
Along with the Gypsy laddie.'

'I could sail the seas with my Jockie Faa,
I could sail the seas with my dearie;
I could sail the seas with my Jockie Faa,
And with pleasure could drown with my dearie.'

They wandered high, they wandered low,
They wandered late and early,
Until they came to an old tenant's barn,
And by this time she was weary.

'Last night I lay in a weel-made bed,
And my noble lord beside me,
And now I must lie in an old tenant's barn,
And the black crew glowering owre me.'

'O hold your tongue, my hinny and my heart,
O hold your tongue, my dearie,
For I will swear, by the moon and the stars,
That thy lord shall nae mair come near thee.'

They wandered high, they wandered low,
They wandered late and early,
Until they came to that wan water,
And by this time she was weary.

'Aften have I rode that wan water,
And my Lord Cassilis beside me,
And now I must set in my white feet and wade,
And carry the Gypsy laddie.'

By and by came home this noble lord,
And asking for his ladie,
The one did cry, the other did reply,
'She is gone with the Gypsy laddie.'

'Go saddle to me the black,' he says,
'The brown rides never so speedie,
And I will neither eat nor drink
Till I bring home my ladie.'

He wandered high, he wandered low,
He wandered late and early,
Until he came to that wan water,
And there he spied his ladie.

'O wilt thou go home, my hinny and my heart,
O wilt thou go home, my dearie?
And I will close thee in a close room,
Where no man shall come near thee.'

'I will not go home, my hinny and my heart,
I will not go home, my dearie;
If I have brewn good beer, I will drink of the same,
And my lord shall nae mair come near me.'

'But I will swear, by the moon and the stars,
And the sun that shines so clearly,
That I am as free of the Gypsy gang
As the hour my mother did bear me.'

They were fifteen valiant men,
Black, but very bonny,
And they lost all their lives for one,
The Earl of Cassillis' ladie.

Traditional